THE LIBRARY OF
HIP-HOP
BIOGRAPHIES™

The Beastie Boys

Thomas Forget

The Rosen Publishing Group, Inc., New York

To my brother Jason, who loves hip-hop more than anyone I know.

Published in 2006 by The Rosen Publishing Group, Inc.
29 East 21st Street, New York, NY 10010

Library of Congress Cataloging-in-Publication Data

Forget, Thomas.
The Beastie Boys/Thomas Forget. — 1st ed.
    p. cm. — (The library of hip-hop biographies)
Includes bibliographical references (p.   ) and discography (p.   ).
ISBN 1-4042-0519-5 (library binding)
1. Beastie Boys. 2. Rap musicians–United States–Biography.
I. Title. II. Series.
ML421.B39F67 2006
782.42164'092'2–dc22

                                                    2005014916

Manufactured in the United States of America

On the cover: The Beastie Boys strike a pose for a photographer in Paris. The picture was taken about a month before the June 2004 release of their most recent album, *To the 5 Boroughs.*

CONTENTS

INTRODUCTION

Adam Yauch, Adam Horovitz, and Michael Diamond. They sound like nice boys, don't they? Like maybe you knew them at camp, or they played on your YMCA basketball team. Well, they have some other names, too. To most of the world, they're known individually as MCA, Adrock, and Mike D. Together, they're famous for being the pioneering hip-hop act the Beastie Boys.

Working in the world of hip-hop, which does not guarantee long careers for even the best rappers, the Beastie Boys have defied the norm for more than twenty years. In 2006, they're just as popular and adventurous as ever. From their humble beginnings as a hardcore punk-rock band, to their multiplatinum debut as white America's ambassadors to the streets, to their current status as mature elder statesmen, the Beastie Boys have always done their best to start the trends and shape the landscape of hip-hop.

The Beastie Boys have survived as long as they have by never turning off their ears or their brains and by refusing to settle on one style or one sound. They've taken bits and pieces of punk, metal, old-school rap, funk, reggae, jazz, and soul to create a musical Frankenstein's monster with every album they've released. Also, unlike many groups in rap, they've mastered both the fine art of sampling other records and playing their own live instruments.

The Beastie Boys have been part of hip-hop since its very beginning in New York City, and have done as much as anyone else in the industry to bring the sounds they love out to the rest of the country. Even though they were the first white faces in a field that was otherwise African American, most people forget that they were not latecomers but started off right there with the rest of the pioneers. The Beastie Boys love hip-hop, and for two decades hip-hop has been very good to them.

CHAPTER ONE

HARDCORE ILLIN'

The story of the Beastie Boys reflects the music scene of New York City toward the end of the twentieth century. In the late 1970s, when the Beastie Boys were growing up, New York experienced an explosion of new music, both in the popular dance clubs of disco and in the brand-new sensation of punk rock.

Punk was a catchall name for a group of rock-and-roll bands committed to working outside of the system of big record companies and commercial radio. Bands like the Ramones, Blondie, Talking Heads, and Television, while not really sounding

alike, were lumped together because of their like-minded ways of making raw music that made personal or artistic statements. Punk was never about getting rich; it was about making something exciting.

From that initial explosion of new music came hundreds of other bands. Lower Manhattan was suddenly flooded with fledgling punk musicians. For the first time in a while, it seemed like anyone at all could be a rock star. You didn't have to be rich or good looking. You didn't even have to be talented, really. You just had to have the drive to say something and have a couple of bucks for a guitar.

While some groups, like Talking Heads, became more interested in creating popular music and experimenting with new sounds, a whole other wing of punk broke off, following the loud, fast rules of Queens, New York's Ramones. These bands turned up the heat, playing faster, playing harder, and screaming louder. The music was called hardcore, and groups like Washington, D.C.'s Minor Threat and Bad Brains perfected the sound in its infancy. Hardcore was raw and heavy, and to most adults over the age of thirty or so, it probably sounded like a whole lot of noise. To kids who were looking to rebel, it was the answer.

BOYS' LIFE

All three of the Beastie Boys were raised in upper-middle-class households in New York City. Adam Yauch, the son of an architect and public school administrator, was born in 1964 and

7

raised in Brooklyn Heights. Michael Diamond, born in 1965, was the son of an art dealer and an interior designer. He grew up in a duplex apartment on Central Park West in Manhattan. Adam Horovitz, born in 1966, was the son of a playwright, Israel Horovitz, and grew up on Eleventh Street in Manhattan's West Village. Despite being from different neighborhoods, all three were drawn together by the pull of punk rock.

The first time the Beastie Boys played together was in 1981, at Yauch's seventeenth birthday party. That first lineup had Yauch on bass, Kate Schellenbach, a high school friend of the boys', on drums, and John Berry on guitar. Mike Diamond sang. That year, they played shows all around New York, opening for bands like Bad Brains (who had moved to New York from Washington, D.C.). The band's early sound was typical for New York hardcore bands: fast drumming, harsh vocals, and rough, loud guitars.

At one of these shows, a man named Dave Parsons, who ran a small record label called Ratcage, saw the boys play and liked them. He invited them to record for his label, and the result was the *Pollywog Stew* EP. It was ragged and had almost no production values, but it was theirs. The Beastie Boys had become a real band.

PUNK ROCK TO HIP-HOP

At the same time that punk was running wild in lower Manhattan, a completely different but no less important kind of music was making waves in the Bronx. Hip-hop had started out without any help from commercial radio, just as punk had. All it took to make hip-hop was two turntables and a microphone. Before long, rooftop and block parties all over the Bronx and upper Manhattan were dominated by DJs cutting and scratching their records to create new, more interesting beats, and MCs rhyming over it all to get people excited.

Hip-hop wasn't planned out. It started off as something to spice up a party, but it quickly became a new style of music. Because no one was really playing an instrument and there was no traditional singing, many people weren't sure if hip-hop was real music at all. But for urban youth, it was the answer. It was something that was completely theirs and no one else's. Hip-hop spread like wildfire throughout New York City. When the young Beastie Boys heard it, it changed their lives.

By 1983, the Beastie Boys were becoming more and more interested in hip-hop and less interested in punk. Both forms of music were political and rebellious, but hip-hop was almost totally new, and its mystery was still fresh. John Berry had left the group by this time and been replaced by Adam Horovitz, who had been the guitar player for a group called the Young and the Useless. The boys took their love of hip-hop and recorded something very different from their first EP. Called *Cooky Puss*, it was a prank call they placed to Carvel Ice Cream's 800 number played over a hip-hop beat.

As silly as *Cooky Puss* was, the Beastie Boys suddenly found themselves being played in clubs all over the city and on college radio. While their music wasn't quite rap, it certainly wasn't punk either. They were moving on, but into what, they weren't sure.

WHAT'S IN A NAME?

The "Beastie" in the Beastie Boys' name actually stands for something longer. According to the band, it is an acronym for Boys Entering Anarchistic States Towards Internal Excellence. The name reportedly came from original guitarist John Berry, but the Beastie Boys stuck with it after he left.

RICK, RUSSELL, AND DEF JAM

While the Beastie Boys were playing punk and soaking up hip-hop culture, two other young men were making big plans. Rick Rubin was a white heavy-metal fan from Long Island. As a student at New York University, he started DJing at local clubs and playing in his own hard rock band. Inspired by the early songs of rap groups like Run DMC, Rubin started mixing up his own hip-hop beats. He used the 1970s hard rock he grew up on, like Aerosmith and AC/DC, and chopped it up to create hard rocking rap beats. In the early 1980s, he started his own small record label, called Def Jam, out of his dorm room.

Meanwhile, in Hollis, an African American neighborhood in Queens, Russell Simmons was getting his own rap business career started. The older brother of Run DMC member Joseph "Run" Simmons, Simmons was a natural-born businessman. He had started by selling illegal drugs in his neighborhood, but he

A 1985 photo captures legendary music producer Rick Rubin and the Beastie Boys in the early days of their careers (from left to right: MCA, Mike D, Rubin, Adrock). Rubin made music history when he produced Run DMC's 1986 cover version of Aerosmith's "Walk This Way." The song appealed to fans of hip-hop and rock music, and rose to number four on the pop charts. Run DMC became the first rap group to have its video played on MTV.

realized how dangerous that life could be. While attending college, he promoted hip-hop shows and managed up-and-coming rappers such as Kurtis Blow. His Rush management company grew quickly, and with his guidance, Blow became the first rapper signed to a major record label.

Simmons and Rubin met through mutual friends and instantly hit it off. Simmons was shocked to find out that the guy who had produced some of the best rap songs he'd heard was a longhaired white kid from Long Island. The two began a business partnership that would take hip-hop music nationwide, with Rubin producing the records and Simmons handling the business and promotion. With the two of them in control, Def Jam would become *the* hip-hop record label.

DJ DOUBLE R AND THE B BOYS

One night, at a New York City club called the Kitchen, the Beastie Boys were introduced to Rubin. By 1984, Kate Schellenbach had left the band. The Beastie Boys hired Rubin as their new DJ, and he went by the alias DJ Double R. The boys also chose stage names for themselves, with Diamond going by Mike D, Yauch becoming MCA, and Horovitz calling himself Adrock. Simmons wanted to take hip-hop beyond New York City. He knew that a group of young white guys with a rebellious attitude could do just that. He agreed to manage the group, and the Beastie Boys began recording for Def Jam.

The group's first release for Def Jam, in 1984, was a twelve-inch record called "Rock Hard"/"Beastie Groove." At this point, the Beastie Boys consisted of MCA, Mike D, and Adrock. Their new single became a sensation in the New York hip-hop clubs, and the boys played shows with acts such as Kurtis Blow and the Fat Boys.

In 1985, they released another record, "She's On It"/"Slow and Low," which was the first Def Jam release to be distributed through major label Columbia Records. The boys continued to

Adrock, MCA, and Mike D show off their rebellious attitude in a 1985 photograph. While the Beastie Boys' image incorporated some old-school hip-hop, they dressed differently from other rappers. They usually went on stage wearing baseball hats, ripped jeans, and T-shirts. The Beastie Boys would go on tour with Madonna in 1985, with disastrous results.

attract attention throughout the New York music scene. They eventually caught the interest of one of the biggest stars in popular music: Madonna. During a period when the Beastie Boys were cooling off and not really doing too much, Simmons called to tell them that they had been booked to open the entire North American leg of Madonna's huge Like a Virgin tour. The Beastie Boys were about to go nationwide.

THE BLONDE AND THE BEASTIES

The Madonna tour was a disaster for the Beastie Boys. They were booed off the stage every single night by Madonna's confused fans. Their rude and disrespectful lyrics, which were mostly meant as jokes, went over the fans' heads. That same year, however, they appeared on a different tour that was a much better fit. The Raising Hell tour was a traveling show of hip-hop's best and brightest at that time. Headlined by Run DMC, the tour also featured Whodini and future megastar (and Adam Horovitz discovery) LL Cool J.

For many people who went to see the tour, it was their first look at the Beastie Boys. Spectators came away astounded that the group they had heard on records was all young white guys. People at the time had the idea that rap was strictly by and for African Americans. The Beastie Boys smashed that idea to pieces. The Raising Hell tour was a huge success, and the way was clear for the Beastie Boys to take things to the next level: a full-length album.

LICENSED TO ILL

The boys and Rick Rubin recorded the first Beastie Boys LP, *Licensed to Ill*, and released it in 1986. Fueled by its first single,

MCA and Mike D bust out lyrics with the members of Run DMC at a 1987 concert. Run DMC was on top of the world in 1987. The year before, its album *Raising Hell* climbed the *Billboard* charts, peaking at number three. It sold more than 3 million copies, more than any other rap album to date.

"Fight for Your Right," the record sold 50,000 copies in the first month of release alone. "Fight for Your Right" was a parody of bad heavy-metal songs, with ridiculous lyrics about partying hard and ignoring one's parents and teachers. The song was mainly meant as a joke, but many of the teenaged headbangers that it made fun of absolutely loved it. The entire country exploded with Beastie-mania. *Licensed to III* gave the boys hit after hit and made history. It became the first rap album to reach number one on the pop charts and stayed there for an incredible seven weeks.

But it wasn't just white rap fans who were buying *Licensed to III*. At the same time that it experienced success on the pop charts, it also reached number two on the urban charts. African American rap fans were accepting the Beastie Boys. They had the credibility they needed to appeal to both the suburbs and the streets.

When the dust cleared, *Licensed to III* had sold 5 million copies. Kids of all races all over America, whether in Brooklyn or Iowa, were suddenly wearing Adidas sneakers with thick untied laces just like Run DMC, and tuning in to MTV's new show *Yo! MTV Raps*. The Beastie Boys' runaway success inspired many kids from suburban and rural areas to check out releases by LL Cool J, Run DMC, and other hip-hop artists.

Not everyone was so thrilled with these strange new pop stars, however. Parents and moral watchdog groups spoke out strongly against the boys' rude lyrics, claiming they encouraged violence, drug abuse, and poor treatment of women. While many of the lyrics on the *Licensed to III* are crude and juvenile, the Beastie Boys always claimed their lyrics were supposed to be a big joke. They loved rap culture, but they liked making fun of some of its lyrical fixations. To many people, however, joking about sex and violence was the same as supporting it.

FALLING APART

The Beastie Boys launched their first headlining tour in support of *Licensed to Ill*. They approached it just like they did everything else they had done, as an opportunity to have fun and do something outrageous. They had obscene props on stage, drank beer throughout their concerts, and had girls dancing in cages. While they meant it as a silly take on rock-star behavior, they found themselves getting caught up in it. By the end of the tour, the group was exhausted and sick of playing the wild, partying Beastie Boys role, especially MCA.

They had also begun to feel as though Def Jam was treating them unfairly, with Rubin and Simmons keeping the lion's share of the money that the Beastie Boys earned for the company. Their relationship with the two label heads fell apart, and the group started to spend more time away from each other. MCA formed a new rock group called Brooklyn, with members of Bad Brains, and Adrock was spending more and more time in Los Angeles. Even though they were one of the most popular groups in the United States, nobody was sure the Beastie Boys would be around for much longer.

CHAPTER TWO

NEW TOWN, NEW LABEL, BRAND-NEW BEASTIES

The Beastie Boys ended 1987 with the huge success of the Licensed to Ill tour. They were one of America's biggest groups, but they were unhappy. The hard-partying lifestyle of the tour had taken a big toll on the Boys, and being together for so long without a break had started to wear on them. Also, the stress they had been experiencing with Def Jam management left them frustrated. Claiming they were owed millions of dollars, the Beastie Boys wanted out of their contract with Def Jam.

After tons of legal back-and-forth, the Beastie Boys were able to get out of their contract and landed on the Capitol Records label. Adam Horovitz had already been spending time in Los Angeles, Capitol's home, and the boys decided to fly there to record their next record. Since they were no longer willing to work with Rick Rubin, they needed to find a new producer.

THE BROTHERS WORK IT OUT

At the same time, in L.A., an old friend of the boys' from the New York club scene, Mike Simpson, was producing records with his partner, John King. Working under the name the Dust Brothers, they were developing a style of beat-making that included thick layers of samples, tiny snippets of dozens of songs put together to make one. Most rap songs at that point had used a much simpler style of mixing. The Dust Brothers were thinking of each new sound they sampled as a different musical instrument in a symphony.

Once the Beastie Boys heard the Dust Brothers' work, they knew they had their producers. The result of the recording sessions was *Paul's Boutique*. The brand-new sounds of *Paul's* placed it on the cutting edge of hip-hop sampling. Released in 1989, it came hot on the heels of two other albums that stretched the limits of what hip-hop music could be: Public Enemy's *It Takes a Nation of Millions to Hold Us Back*, produced by the Bomb Squad, and De La Soul's *Three Feet High and Rising*, produced by Prince Paul. In a 1989 *Billboard* article by Chris Morris,

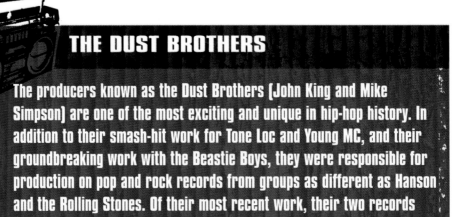

THE DUST BROTHERS

The producers known as the Dust Brothers (John King and Mike Simpson) are one of the most exciting and unique in hip-hop history. In addition to their smash-hit work for Tone Loc and Young MC, and their groundbreaking work with the Beastie Boys, they were responsible for production on pop and rock records from groups as different as Hanson and the Rolling Stones. Of their most recent work, their two records with Beck, *Odelay* and *Guero*, are thought to be among their finest.

Mike D described the record's sound: "You could use the word, maybe 'stew,' or 'pot luck dinner,' or 'casserole,' those type of terms. What you're talking about is, you're combining a lot of different things, a lot of different seasonings."

De La Soul and Public Enemy's records made stars of both groups, but the Beastie Boys, who were already huge, met disappointing sales with *Paul's Boutique*. On the one hand, the same critics who had put the Beastie Boys down as being rude and childish were now praising them, but the public that loved their attitude on *Licensed* were confused by *Paul's*. The lyrics were still full of jokes, but it was a different kind of humor. Instead of the usual bragging about sex and violence, the references ranged from 1970s action movies to writers such as Jack Kerouac. The artists sampled on the album included Johnny Cash, the Eagles, and the

The members of De La Soul mug for the camera in a 1989 photo shoot. De La Soul emerged from a thriving alternative hip-hop scene that included A Tribe Called Quest, the Jungle Brothers, and Leaders of the New School. Their 1989 debut album, *Three Feet High and Rising* contained philosophical and intellectual lyrics and eclectic samples.

Beatles. *Paul's Boutique* was unlike anything that came before it, but instead of celebrating its difference, people didn't buy it.

AHEAD OF THEIR TIME

Paul's Boutique eventually sold 1 million copies, a success for most, but disappointing when compared to *Licensed to Ill* sales.

The Beastie Boys knew they had done something to be proud of, however, and they would get the last laugh. The public eventually caught up with *Paul's Boutique*, and it's now considered one of the most important hip-hop albums of all time. After the record was finished, the boys found themselves in love with Los Angeles and moved there.

The boys also got to work building a recording studio called G-Son. After the limited success of *Paul's*, the Beastie Boys found that they were no longer in the public eye, and they were free to explore their new home and everything it offered. They also found the time to do something they hadn't done in a long time: they picked up their instruments.

CHECK YOUR HEAD

As they started working on their next album, the Beastie Boys realized they had nothing to lose. Because *Paul's* had been ignored by most of the public, they felt that they could try anything. And it turned out that what they wanted to do was play instruments, just like in their punk-rock days. Mike D picked up the drums, MCA got back on the bass, and Adrock got on the guitar. They got together and played long jam sessions, deciding afterward which bits would make a good song. The music they were putting together was still mostly hip-hop, but there were many different flavors in the mix as well.

The resulting album, *Check Your Head*, ended up having live instruments on about 70 percent of the tracks. By this time,

The Beastie Boys perform at a 1992 concert in support of the album *Check Your Head*. The Beastie Boys eschewed samples and drum machines on *Check Your Head*, choosing instead to play live instruments. Audiences loved the group's new direction, and the album went double platinum in the United States alone.

it was 1992, and no one could tell what the public's reaction to a new Beastie Boys record would be. During the three years since *Paul's Boutique*, pop music had changed. With alternative rock groups including Nirvana, R.E.M., and Sonic Youth becoming more and more popular, and rap getting meaner and harder, would there be room for the Beastie Boys?

CHAPTER THREE

RAP AND ROCK ROYALTY

The Beastie Boys prepared to release their new album, *Check Your Head*. The first single was called "Pass the Mic." Right away, buzz started up on the streets. The single was getting airplay not just on rap stations but on alternative rock radio as well. A whole new audience, one not at all different from the kids who would have liked the Beastie Boys' early punk recordings, had picked up on *Paul's Boutique* over the past three years. Skateboarders, punks, and hip-hop fans alike found themselves hungry for more Beastie Boys material. *Check Your Head* was different from the kind of music anyone else was making, and it was a hit.

BEASTIE BOYS DISCOGRAPHY

Pollywog Stew EP – Ratcage Records – 1982
Cooky Puss – Ratcage Records – 1983
Licensed to Ill – Def Jam/CBS – 1986
Paul's Boutique – Capitol Records – 1989
Check Your Head – Grand Royal/Capitol Records – 1992
Ill Communication – Grand Royal/Capitol Records – 1994
Aglio e Olio – Grand Royal/Capitol Records – 1995
Hello Nasty – Grand Royal/Capitol Records – 1998
To the 5 Boroughs – EMI/Capitol Records – 2004

Energized by the thrill of playing live instruments again, and excited by *Check Your Head*'s positive reviews and healthy sales, the Beastie Boys, who had not toured for *Paul's*, launched a major tour in the summer of 1992. The tour was a huge success, and the boys entered a period of amazing popularity. The early 1990s was one of the most adventurous periods in pop music. Rappers like Dr. Dre and Snoop Dogg sat right next to grunge rockers like Soundgarden and Pearl Jam. By combining their rap and punk roots to create something different, the Beastie Boys managed to appeal to fans of both kinds of music. For a while, they were the group that everyone could agree on.

GRAND ROYALTY

Many groups would be satisfied with the album sales and tour success that the Beastie Boys were experiencing by 1993, but the boys wanted more. They didn't just want to produce their own music; they wanted to bring bands that they liked to the public. The result of this need to share was their record label, Grand Royal. The label's first release was Luscious Jackson's *In Search of Manny*. (Luscious Jackson not only toured with the boys but also featured old friend Kate Schellenbach on drums.) Grand Royal would go on to release records by artists as different as folk-rocker Ben Lee and Texas punks At the Drive-In.

Grand Royal wasn't just a record label, however. Later in 1993, the fall/winter issue of *Grand Royal* magazine was launched. The magazine wasn't just about the Beastie Boys. It covered anything that they and their friends had ever been interested in. It was almost like the magazine version of *Paul's Boutique*, in the mixture of what it presented. The first issue featured a cover story on martial arts legend Bruce Lee and interviews with NBA superstar Kareem Abdul-Jabbar and rapper Q-Tip.

ILL COMMUNICATION

Even though they were on top of their game, the Beastie Boys were not ready to settle. They were on a creative hot streak and had way too many ideas to sit on. Plus, their fans wanted more. During the second half of 1993, they began recording another

The Beastie Boys play their instruments during a rehearsal for the 1994 MTV Video Music Awards show at Radio City Music Hall in New York City. MCA is on the bass to the left, Adrock is singing while playing guitar, and Mike D keeps the beat in the back. The video for *III Communication*'s "Sabotage" received heavy airplay on MTV.

album. They were still continuing in the style of *Check Your Head*, with live instruments and samples, and a mixture of rap, funk, and punk, but they were determined to push things further.

With *Check Your Head*'s Mario Caldato Jr. producing again, they began experimenting with new, unusual equipment. They used broken microphones and speakers, toy mics, and even a karaoke machine to create a certain kind of voice distortion. On fire creatively, the band ripped through the recording, finishing the

SPIKE JONZE

Music video director Spike Jonze ruled 1990s alternative rock. His playful and innovative videos for groups as different as the Beastie Boys, Pharcyde, Weezer, and the Notorious B.I.G. completely changed the face of MTV. After getting his start as a skateboarding photographer, he began filming the skaters for videos, gradually moving into music video. He made the leap into feature film in 1999, with the Oscar-nominated *Being John Malkovitch* and the also-nominated *Adaptation* in 2002.

record in seven months. The sound was more extreme than *Check Your Head*. The punk sounds were faster and harder, the funk instrumentals were wild, and the samples included bits of jazz flute and Buddhist monk chants. Called *Ill Communication*, it was even more successful than *Check Your Head*.

One of the main reasons for the popularity of *Ill Communication* was the smash lead single, "Sabotage," bolstered by its hilarious video. Directed by future Oscar nominee Spike Jonze, it shows the Beastie Boys dressed as 1970s plainclothes cops, just like in gritty 1970s TV shows like *Streets of San Francisco* and *Starsky and Hutch*. The boys and Jonze did their research, watching the shows to learn the right attitude and style of dress. The research paid off. "Sabotage" is still considered one of the funniest and most original videos ever filmed.

Headlining at the 1994 Lollapalooza tour, the Beastie Boys command the stage. Lollapalooza was a traveling outdoor music festival that was started in 1991 . An extremely popular festival, Lollapalooza featured alternative rock, punk music, and rap. The Beastie Boys' success headlining Lollapalooza set the stage for the benefit concerts they would organize in the years to come.

THE BOYS GIVE BACK

The success of *Ill Communication* did not just benefit the Beastie Boys. The royalties for two of the songs on the record, "Bodhisattva Vow" and "Shambala," were donated to the Milarepa Fund, a nonprofit organization dedicated to promoting awareness of the injustices committed by the Chinese government against the citizens of Tibet. Communist China conquered Tibet in the 1950s, and the citizens lost most of their freedoms, including the right to practice their form of Buddhism.

MCA first became interested in the problems of Tibet while on a snowboarding trip. His interest grew into a passion, as he found beauty and peace in practicing the Tibetan Buddhist religion. The boys found themselves in a place where young people wanted to hear what they had to say, and they could not keep silent about something that disturbed them so much. They had come a long way from the hard-partying boys who recorded *Licensed to Ill*.

Their commitment to helping free Tibet also included three concerts, one each in Los Angeles, New York, and Washington, D.C., with all money going to the Milarepa Fund. The Beastie Boys worked hard to keep their fans educated about what was going on in Tibet, and they also began to speak out against violence toward women. In the summer of 1994, they got the perfect opportunity to bring their music and message to the people, when they were asked to headline the alternative rock supertour Lollapalooza.

At that time, Lollapalooza was the absolute height of cool. By headlining, the Beastie Boys were seen as the coolest of the cool. People knew what a dynamic live show they put on. In 1995, when they launched their next tour, the Quadrophonic Joystick Action arena tour, shows were selling out in as little as twenty minutes. They continued to follow their conscience, with one dollar from each ticket sold going to the Milarepa Fund. At a time when most Americans had no idea what the people of Tibet were going through, the Beastie Boys were using their fame to make it known. But their work was not yet complete.

CHAPTER FOUR
NEW YORKERS NOW AND FOREVER

The Beastie Boys closed out 1995 on top of the world. Their recent tour was a major success, with a chunk of the ticket sales going to help free Tibet. They were one of the most widely respected bands in the country, with fans of all races and from all walks of life. It had been a very busy couple of years, and the group finished up 1995 with a quick, vicious punk EP, *Aglio e Olio*, featuring eight songs in eleven minutes. After that, they began a well-earned period of rest.

FREEDOM ROCK

While they were taking it easy compared to recent years, 1996 featured the start of something very important to the boys. On June 15 and 16, they organized and performed in the first Tibetan Freedom Concert, a huge festival at the Polo Fields in San Francisco's Golden Gate Park. The enormous scale of the festival made it the largest benefit concert since 1985's Live Aid concert, with 100,000 people showing up for two days of music and politics. Performers included rap groups De La Soul and A Tribe Called Quest, blues musicians John Lee Hooker and Buddy Guy, and alternative rockers like the Red Hot Chili Peppers and the Smashing Pumpkins. The festival also included political speakers and Buddhist scholars.

The Tibetan Freedom Concert became an annual event, helping to raise awareness for what is still a big problem for native Tibetans. In 1998, the concert sold out, with 130,000 people attending, in one afternoon. The magnitude and importance of the concerts showed just how much the Beastie Boys had grown.

HOMEBOYS

In 1997, the Beastie Boys took another big step. After almost a decade in Los Angeles, they decided to return to their roots and relocate to New York City. The city's rich hip-hop history and the arrival of a new DJ, Mixmaster Mike, inspired them to put their

The Beastie Boys perform at the first Tibetan Freedom Concert in San Francisco in 1996. The Milarepa Fund, founded in 1994, is devoted to helping the people of Tibet, who are currently controlled by the People's Republic of China. China took control of Tibet in the 1950s, forcing Tibet's government, led by the fourteenth Dalai Lama, into exile.

instruments down and record a more sample-based record. The mixture of different musical styles that they used on earlier records was still there, but now it was built through layers of samples, closer to the way they worked on *Paul's Boutique*.

The new album, called *Hello Nasty*, was released on July 14, 1998. The wild mixture of sounds included the usual funk and hip-hop, but it also introduced easy listening, electronica, and soul. The Beastie Boys' raps were delivered in their usual old-school

The Beastie Boys put down their instruments for 1998's innovative *Hello Nasty*. The album featured layers of samples and was a huge hit with fans and critics.

trade-off style, as pioneered by Run DMC, but were surrounded with unusual electronic beeps and whirrs, giving *Hello Nasty* a surprisingly futuristic sound. After two albums of looking back at the funk of the 1970s, the boys were determined to take classic rap and bring it into the next century.

Hello Nasty was another instant success, showing that the time off had not affected their fans' love for the group one bit. It sold 700,000 copies in its first week alone, and it went to number one all over the world.

THE VICTORY LAP

In 1999, the boys sat back and collected the praise for *Hello Nasty*. They were honored by major magazines like *Spin* and *Rolling Stone* with record-, artist-, or band-of-the-year awards. At the Grammys that year, they won the prize for best hip-hop performance by a duo or group for their single "Intergalactic" and best alternative music performance for *Hello Nasty*. It was the first time an artist had ever won in both categories, and only the Beastie Boys, with their refusal to stay in one musical box, could have pulled it off.

After such a long and varied career, the Beastie Boys took a minute to take stock of their music, then released a two-CD anthology followed by a two-disc DVD.

The boys were planning a special tour to celebrate the CD and DVD releases for 2000, but Mike D suffered a serious injury while riding his bicycle. Due to his surgery and long periods of physical therapy, the tour had to be cancelled. It was grim news, but shortly after, something much more serious would crash into the Beastie Boys' and all of their fellow New Yorkers' worlds.

9/11 HITS HOME

The terrorist attacks of September 11, 2001, affected every single American in some way. As native New Yorkers, the Beastie Boys were devastated by what happened to their home. They had spent great amounts of time and effort over the past ten years helping the citizens of Tibet. Now they were ready to bring their experience in organizing artists for charity to help their own friends and neighbors in New York. Working through the Milarepa Fund, the boys struck quickly, headlining the New Yorkers Against Violence benefit on October 28 and 29 at New York's Hammerstein Ballroom.

The lineup for the benefit was a who's who of New York City all-stars, including the Strokes, the B-52's, and Mos Def,

Mike D and Adrock trade off a verse during the New Yorkers Against Violence concert at New York's Hammerstein Ballroom. Organized by the Beastie Boys, New Yorkers Against Violence raised money in the wake of the September 11, 2001, terrorist attacks. In 2004, the Beastie Boys would release *To the 5 Boroughs*, a tribute to their hometown.

with special appearances by Moby, R.E.M.'s Michael Stipe, U2's Bono, and Yoko Ono. Though there were many different charities they could have given the money to, the boys chose the New York Women's Foundation Disaster Relief Fund and the New York Association for New Americans.

TO THE 5 BOROUGHS

In 2002, the boys, who had left behind their G-Son recording studio in Los Angeles, built a new studio, Oscilloscope, in downtown Manhattan. With the new studio in place and an urgent need to say something after 9/11, the Beastie Boys began recording their first new material in four years. For their new record, they were moved by the power of hip-hop as a force to help people get through hard times. With New York facing one of its darkest periods in decades, the Beastie Boys could think of no better way to help their city, and Americans all over, than to create an old-fashioned hip-hop party record.

By the middle of the following year, word of a new Beastie Boys album had fans foaming at the mouth. There had never been a gap that wide between records, and people wondered what this ever-changing group was going to do next. In March 2003, they made "In a World Gone Mad," a vicious but funny attack on the George W. Bush administration and its plans for war, available for download on their own and several political Web sites. It was a sign that the Beastie Boys were not going to be quiet, even if they had to take on the president.

The finished album, *To the 5 Boroughs*, contained a mix of the political content of "In a World Gone Mad" and a warm celebration of the city of New York and its hip-hop culture. For the first time, the boys produced themselves, whipping up a mix of classic party beats. Bits and pieces of rap songs from the very start of the boys' career made appearances, bridging the gap from the dawn of hip-hop to the present day. Intended as a love letter to their home as well as a tonic to heal its wounds, *Boroughs* looks back at all of the break-dancers, DJs, MCs, and clubs that built a city of hip-hop at the end of the hard 1970s. It reminds people to stand up and dance, despite all of their problems.

To the 5 Boroughs' June 15, 2004, release brought about a swarm of Beastie Boys activity. After keeping a low profile for the past few years, the boys were greeted enthusiastically by the public. *Boroughs* debuted at number one, selling close to 400,000 copies in its first week. Most reviews were positive. People liked the old-school sound and were impressed by the boys' work with the talented Mix Master Mike.

BOYS TO MEN

Today, the Beastie Boys have nothing left to prove. With a career that has lasted as long as hip-hop itself and the popularity to be considered music legends, they could easily sit back and play golf for the rest of their years. But with too few people willing to put their necks on the line, both artistically and politically, the world continues to need the Beastie Boys. Even though two of them are parents and there have been rumors that a breakup is coming, it's hard to believe that they would be willing to part ways with their longtime love of hip-hop. They can't, they won't, and they don't stop.

The Beastie Boys arrive at the 2004 MTV Video Music Awards Latin America in Miami Beach, Florida, on October 21, 2004. They have integrated many different influences into their sonic mix, and have found consistent success and a loyal fan base. One of the most unique products of the hip-hop movement, the Beastie Boys have been around for more than twenty years and show no signs of stopping.

TIMELINE

1981 The Beastie Boys, then consisting of Michael Diamond (vocals), Adam Yauch (bass), Kate Schellenbach (drums), and John Berry (guitar), play their first show at Yauch's seventeenth birthday party.

1982 The first Beastie Boys lineup records and releases the *Pollywog Stew* seven-inch.

1983 Adam Horovitz replaces John Berry. The group records the *Cooky Puss* twelve-inch, its first attempt at hip-hop.

1984 The Mike D, MCA, and Adrock Beastie Boys lineup debuts with the "Rock Hard"/"Beastie Groove" twelve-inch.

1986 *Licensed to Ill*, the first Beastie Boys full-length, is released. It is the first rap album to go number one on the pop charts.

1989 The group releases its second album, *Paul's Boutique*. It is not as commercially successful as its debut, but it is hailed as a masterpiece by critics.

1992 *Check Your Head*, the group's third album, is released. Featuring live instruments and an experimental sound, it is a major success, going double platinum and leading to a popular tour.

1993 Grand Royal, the group's record label, with its accompanying magazine, are founded.

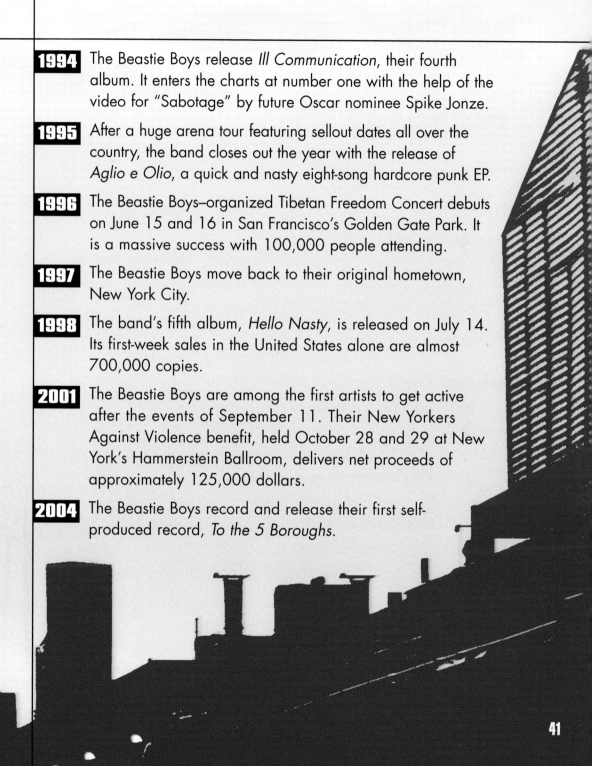

1994 The Beastie Boys release *Ill Communication*, their fourth album. It enters the charts at number one with the help of the video for "Sabotage" by future Oscar nominee Spike Jonze.

1995 After a huge arena tour featuring sellout dates all over the country, the band closes out the year with the release of *Aglio e Olio*, a quick and nasty eight-song hardcore punk EP.

1996 The Beastie Boys–organized Tibetan Freedom Concert debuts on June 15 and 16 in San Francisco's Golden Gate Park. It is a massive success with 100,000 people attending.

1997 The Beastie Boys move back to their original hometown, New York City.

1998 The band's fifth album, *Hello Nasty*, is released on July 14. Its first-week sales in the United States alone are almost 700,000 copies.

2001 The Beastie Boys are among the first artists to get active after the events of September 11. Their New Yorkers Against Violence benefit, held October 28 and 29 at New York's Hammerstein Ballroom, delivers net proceeds of approximately 125,000 dollars.

2004 The Beastie Boys record and release their first self-produced record, *To the 5 Boroughs*.

GLOSSARY

cutting Scratching a record to create a beat or to play a certain part of the song.

DJ Short for "disc jockey," the DJ handles the turntables, creating the backing music in hip-hop.

EP Short for "extended player," a record with more than one song but with fewer songs than a full-length. An EP generally contains around six to eight songs.

funk Music that combines traditional African American forms, such as soul and blues, with a strong backbeat.

grunge Rough hard rock indebted both to the simplicity of punk and the huge sound of 1970s heavy metal.

hardcore A faster, louder form of punk rock.

hip-hop A form of music pioneered in urban, primarily African American communities. Hip-hop is created by using prerecorded music and rarely contains live instrumentation.

jazz An American form of music that prominently uses horns in ensemble-based playing.

LP Short for "long player," a full-length album of songs.

MC Originally short for "master of ceremonies." In hip-hop, the MC rhymes over beats.

metal A rough, heavy form of hard rock.

old-school Relating to the original or first of something.

parody A close imitation of something designed to make fun of it.

platinum A designation given to an album that has sold 1 million copies.

punk A genre of rock music characterized by a fast, abrasive style, usually dealing with subjects relating to social discontent.

rap To rhyme in rhythm over a DJ's beats.

reggae Jamaican form of music that combines native sounds with American soul and rhythm 'n' blues.

sample A small part of a song used as a part of the music for a new song.

scratching Moving a record back and forth on the turntable.

seven-inch A small record measuring seven inches that usually contains a song on each side.

soul A passionate African American form of music originating from gospel and blues.

twelve-inch A record measuring twelve inches that can contain one longer song or several songs on each side.

FOR MORE INFORMATION

The Milarepa Fund
P.O. Box 1678
New York, NY 10013
Web site: http://www.milarepa.org/

Capitol Records
1750 N. Vine St.
Los Angeles, CA 90028-5209
(323) 462-6252
Web site: http://www.capitolrecords.com

Web Sites

Due to the changing nature of Internet links, the Rosen Publishing Group, Inc., has developed an online list of Web sites related to the subject of this book. This site is updated regularly. Please use this link to access the list:

http://www.rosenlinks.com/lhhb/bebo

FOR FURTHER READING

Haskins, Jim. *One Nation Under a Groove: Rap Music and Its Roots*. New York, NY: Jump at the Sun, 2000.

Heatley, Michael. *Beastie Boys: In Their Own Words*. London, England: Omnibus Press, 1999.

Jones, Maurice K. *Say It Loud!: The Story of Rap Music*. New York, NY: Millbrook Press, 1994.

Lommel, Cookie. *The History of Rap Music* (African-American Achievers). New York, NY: Chelsea House Publications, 2003.

BIBLIOGRAPHY

Hamersly, Michael. "Beastie Boys Tackle Politics, Big Apple Pride on New Record." Retrieved March 14, 2005 (http://www.beaconnewspaper.com).

Jenison, David. "Beasties Ch-Check in at No. 1." Retrieved March 5, 2005 (http://www.eonline.com).

Loder, Kurt. "Beastie Boys: Big Fat Liars." Retrieved February 28, 2005 (http://www.mtv.com/bands/b/beastie_boys/news_feature_040517/).

Rocco, John, ed. *The Beastie Boys Companion: Two Decades of Commentary* (The Companion Series). New York, NY: Schirmer Books, 1999.

Simmons, Russel, with Neslon George. *Life and Def: Sex, Drugs, Money, and God.* New York, NY: Three Rivers Press, 2002.

INDEX

About the Author

Thomas Forget lives in Brooklyn, New York, where one of the three Beastie Boys grew up. He bought *Check Your Head* the day it came out and saw the Beastie Boys on their 1992 tour when he was fourteen years old.

Photo Credits

Cover, pp. 29, 33, 36 © Getty Images, Inc.; p. 1 © Bertrand Guay/AFP/Getty Images, Inc.; p. 11 © Photofest; p. 13 © Glen E. Friedman/The Everett Collection; p. 15 © Neal Preston/Corbis; p. 21 © Paul Natkin/WireImage.com; p. 23 © Steve Eichner/PhotoWeb/WireImage.com; p. 27 © AP/Wide World Photos; p. 34 © Time Life Pictures/Getty Images, Inc.; p. 38 © Bill Davila/Reuters/Corbis.

Designer: Thomas Forget